Deliciously Easy
SALADS and SAUCES

WITH

HERBS

DAWN J. RANCK and
PHYLLIS PELLMAN GOOD

Good Books

Intercourse, PA 17534

Cover design and illustration by Cheryl Benner
Design by Dawn J. Ranck
Illustrations by Cheryl Benner

DELICIOUSLY EASY SALADS AND SAUCES WITH HERBS
Copyright © 1998 by Good Books, Intercourse, Pennsylvania, 17534
International Standard Book Number: 1-56148-256-0
Library of Congress Catalog Card Number: 98-41502

Library of Congress Cataloging-in-Publication Data
Ranck, Dawn J.
       Deliciously easy salads and sauces with herbs / Dawn J.
Ranck and Phyllis Pellman Good.
       p. cm. -- (Deliciously easy -- with herbs)
ISBN 1-56148-256-0
1. Salads. 2. Salad dressing. 3. Cookery (Herbs) I. Good, Phyllis
Pellman. II. Title. III. Series: Ranck, Dawn J.
Deliciously easy -- with herbs.
TX740.R346 1998
641.8'3--dc21   98-41502
                                                                            CIP

Table of Contents

Tomato Summer Salad

Kelly Stelzer
Elderflower Farm
Roseburg, OR

Makes 4 servings

4 large tomatoes
3 tsp. olive oil
1¹/2 Tbsp. fresh lemon juice
1 tsp. grated lemon peel
¹/2 tsp. freshly ground
  black pepper
salt to taste (optional)
¹/2 cup chopped fresh parsley

¹/4 cup chopped
  green onions
¹/2 cup chopped red or
  yellow bell peppers
1 cup cooked rice,
  mixed with
  ¹/4 tsp. saffron threads

1. Hollow out tomatoes and set shells aside. Save ¹/4 cup of the pulp.
2. Mix together ¹/4 cup tomato pulp, olive oil, lemon juice, lemon peel, pepper, and salt.
3. Mix together parsley, onions, peppers, and rice. Add tomato dressing and toss to coat vegetable/rice ingredients well.
4. Stuff tomatoes with rice mixture. Serve at room temperature.

Tomato and Mozzarella Salad

Jacoba Baker & Reenie Baker Sandsted
Baker's Acres
Groton, NY

Makes 4-6 servings

2 fresh ripe medium tomatoes,
  cored, and cut into ¹/4" slices
¹/2 cup packed fresh basil,
  washed and drained
2 Tbsp. olive oil

1 tsp. fresh lemon juice
¹/4 tsp. salt
¹/2 lb. mozzarella,
  cut into ¹/4" slices

1. Arrange tomato slices in single layer on paper towel and let drain for 15 minutes.
2. Place basil, oil, lemon juice, and salt in blender. Blend on low speed until basil is finely chopped.

3. Arrange tomato and mozzarella slices overlapping in alternate rows on large platter. Drizzle with basil sauce.
4. Cover loosely, and let stand at room temperature for 30 minutes before serving.

Marinated Tomatoes

Lewis J. Matt III
White Buck Farm
Holbrook, PA

Makes 4 servings

2 large tomatoes, sliced
2 thin slices from center
   of large sweet onion
clove of garlic, thinly sliced
   in julienne strips
1/4 cup chopped fresh basil
   (5 tsp. dried)
1/4 cup chopped fresh parsley
   (5 tsp. dried)

1/4 tsp. chopped fresh lemon
   thyme (pinch of dried)
1 cup balsamic vinegar
1/4 cup olive oil
1/2 tsp. freshly ground
   pepper

1. Arrange tomatoes and onion on a plate.
2. Mix together remaining ingredients. Pour over tomatoes.
3. Cover with plastic wrap and refrigerate overnight.

Herby Tomato and Cucumber Salad

Lorraine Hamilton
Lorraine's Herb Garden
Neelyton, PA

Makes 6-8 servings

2 medium-sized ripe tomatoes,
cut in 3/4" chunks
1 medium-sized onion,
cut in 1/4" chunks
1 medium-sized cucumber,
cut in 1/2" chunks
8 oz. mozzarella cheese,
shredded

3 Tbsp. olive oil
3 Tbsp. herb vinegar
(chive, basil, or flower)
1/3 cup chopped fresh herb
flowers—choose chive,
basil, oregano, or a
combination of any of
those
herb flowers for garnish

1. Toss together tomatoes, onions, cucumbers, and cheese.
2. Drizzle oil and vinegar over vegetable mixture. Toss.
3. Add herb flowers and toss well.
4. Refrigerate for 1 hour. Garnish with additional fresh herb flowers and serve.

Sweet and Sour Cucumbers

Connie Butto
The Herb Shop
Lititz, PA

Makes 6 servings

3 medium cucumbers
1/4 cup sugar
1/2 cup cider vinegar
1/4 cup water

1/2 tsp. salt
1/4 tsp. coarsely ground
black pepper
1 Tbsp. minced parsley

1. Peel cucumbers, and then score them lengthwise with fork. Slice very thin. Put on paper towels and blot dry.
2. Mix together sugar, vinegar, water, salt, pepper, and parsley. Add cucumbers and toss lightly.
3. Chill for several hours before serving.

Sudanese Cucumbers

Mary Peddie
The Herb Market
Washington, KY

Makes 6 servings

2 cups plain yogurt
1 cup finely chopped fresh mint
5 small cucumbers

salt
juice of lemon or lime

1. Mix together yogurt and mint. Cover and chill for several
   hours.
2. Slice cucumbers very thin. Salt lightly and place in refrigerator
   to chill. When cucumbers "wilt," rinse them in icy water and
   drain well.
3. Just before serving, add lemon to yogurt mixture. Pour over
   cucumbers. Toss gently to coat. Serve immediately.

Cucumbers with Dill

Barbara Steele & Marlene Lueriu
Alloway Gardens & Herb Farm
Littlestown, PA

Makes 6 servings

2 cups thinly sliced cucumbers
1/2 cup sour cream
2 tsp. vinegar
1/2 tsp. sugar
2 tsp. chopped fresh chives
2 tsp. chopped fresh dill

Mix together all ingredients. Chill
   several hours before serving.

Moroccan Cucumbers

Linda Jani and Chris Aylesworth
Viewhurst Farm Herb & Garden Shop
Hebron, IN

Makes 6 servings

2 large cucumbers
1/2 cup white wine vinegar,
  or white wine vinegar with
  mint and lemon balm

1/2 cup sugar
pinch of salt
1/4 cup chopped fresh mint
  leaves (5 tsp. dried)

1. Peel and slice cucumbers.
2. Mix together vinegar, sugar, and salt until sugar is dissolved.
3. Pour over sliced cucumbers. Mix well.
4. Chill for one hour before serving. Garnish with chopped mint.

Mint Salad

Judith M. Graves
Lambs & Thyme at Randallano
Richmond, NH

Makes 4-6 servings

1 head lettuce, broken into
  bite-sized pieces
1/2 cup shredded carrots
1/2 cup lightly cooked peas
1/2 cup chopped fresh mint
1/2 cup vegetable oil

1/4 cup mint vinegar
  (see page 9)
1/4 cup chopped almonds
  or walnuts
1/4 cup raisins

1. Toss together lettuce, carrots, peas, and mint.
2. Whisk oil, vinegar, nuts, and raisins together. Pour over salad. Toss. Serve immediately.

8

Mint Vinegar

Judith M. Graves
Lambs and Thyme at Randallone
Richmond, NH

Makes 1 quart

mint leaves
1 quart white wine vinegar,
   or apple cider vinegar
fresh mint sprig

1. Fill quart jar with mint leaves. Fill with vinegar.
2. Let stand in unlit area for 2-3 weeks.
3. Strain vinegar into fresh bottle. Discard mint leaves. Add a
   fresh sprig of mint to bottle for identification.

Clarence's Basil Salad

Marty Mertens & Clarence Roush
Woodstock Herbs
New Goshen, IN

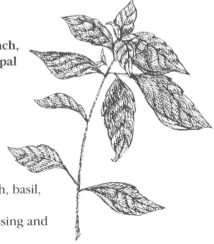

1 sweet onion, sliced in rings
salad greens, mixed in these
    proportions: 1/3 fresh spinach,
    1/3 fresh basil (green and opal
    mixed for color), 1/3 red
    leaf lettuce
Italian dressing, or
    mixture of herbed or
    balsamic vinegar and
    olive oil

1. Toss together onion, spinach, basil,
   and lettuce.
2. Add desired amount of dressing and
   toss well.

Grapefruit Grandeur

Carol Turner
Turkey Trot Trunk
Mountain City, GA

Makes 4 servings

4 large handfuls seasonal greens
2 grapefruit, sectioned*

1 red or green bell pepper,
cut in rings

Dressing:
1/4 cup olive oil
1/4 cup reserved grapefruit juice
1 tsp. balsamic vinegar

1 Tbsp. chopped fresh
parsley (1 tsp. dried)
1 Tbsp. chopped fresh
rosemary (1 tsp. dried)

1. Arrange a handful of salad greens on each plate.
   Top with grapefruit sections and rings of bell
   pepper.
2. Mix together dressing ingredients. Sprinkle
   over each salad before serving.

* To section a grapefruit easily, cut off its top
   and bottom. Place on cutting board and cut
   skin in strips, exposing fruit, then insert
   knife in one side of dividing membrane
   and flip out secions, one at a time.

Tasty and Colorful Garden Salad

Diane T. Morris
The Morris Farm
Seaboard, NC

lettuce leaves
tomato, chopped
cucumber, sliced
onion, sliced
parsley in bite-sized pieces
basil leaves
chive blossoms

lovage leaves and stems
cilantro leaves and blooms
thyme leaves and blooms
dill leaves and blooms
1/3 cup opal basil vinegar
2/3 cup mayonnaise

1. Mix together lettuce, tomato, cucumber, onion, and other salad ingredients.
2. Add all or some herbs.
3. Mix together vinegar and mayonnaise (it will be pink) and serve with salad.

Greek Salad

Harriette Johnson &
Dianna Johnson-Fiergola
Mustard Seed Herbs & Everlastings
Spring Valley, WI

Makes 8 servings

1 lb. rotini, cooked
1 3/4-2 cups kidney beans, drained
1 3/4-2 cups garbanzo beans, drained
1 cup black olives, drained and sliced
1 pt. cherry tomatoes, cut in half

1 bunch green onions, sliced
2 cucumbers, diced
1 lb. feta cheese, crumbled
coarse black pepper to taste
salt to taste
1/4-1/2 cup herbal flavored vinegar, to taste

Gently toss together all ingredients.

Pasta Salad

Donna Treloar
Harmony
Gaston, IN

Makes 12-20 servings,
depending on the number and amount of ingredients

1 pkg. (12 or 16 oz.) angel-hair
  pasta, fettuccini,
  or thin vermicelli
1 cup Harmony Italian Dressing
  (following)
Any or all of the following
  (to taste):
  green onions,
    sliced with tops
  diced red onion
  diced green, red, or
    gold peppers
  fresh ripe tomatoes, diced
    (or a can of drained, diced
    tomatoes, if preparing salad
    out of tomato season)

sliced black olives
diced water chestnuts
grated cheese (cheddar,
  Colby, or Parmesan)
frozen peas or small pea pods
chopped raw broccoli
  or cauliflower
grated or diced zucchini
chopped celery
sliced mushrooms
poppy or caraway seeds

1. Cook pasta according to package directions. Do not overcook!
   Drain and rinse with cold water.
2. Toss dressing with pasta. Cut through pasta several times with
   a sharp knife. Cover and refrigerate.
3. Mix together selection of remaining ingredients to your liking.
   Mix with pasta. Add more dressing as needed. Cover and
   refrigerate for at least 8 hours.

Note: This makes a large amount to take to carry-ins and pic-
nics. It keeps well in the refrigerator and gets better with age.

Variation 1: Add tuna or chicken.

Variation 2: Add 3/4 cup mayonnaise to Italian dressing.

Harmony Italian Dressing

Donna Treloar
Harmony
Gaston, IN

Makes 1 1/2 cups

1 cup olive oil
1/2 cup red wine vinegar,
   or your choice
1 1/2 tsp. chopped fresh basil
   (1/2 tsp. dried)

1 1/2 tsp. chopped fresh
   oregano (1/2 tsp. dried)
1 clove garlic, minced,
   or 1/2 tsp. garlic powder
freshly ground pepper
   to taste

1. Mix together all ingredients in jar with lid. Shake well.
2. Let stand for several days before using to allow flavors to blend.
3. Store in refrigerator.

German Potato Salad

Kelly Stelzer
Elderflower Farm
Roseburg, OR

Makes 4-6 servings

1 1/2 lbs. small red potatoes
1/4 cup rice or wine vinegar
1 Tbsp. sugar
1 Tbsp. prepared mustard
1/2 cup plain yogurt
1/2 cup mayonnaise
2 slices bacon, cooked,
   drained, and crumbled

3/4 cup green onions,
   chopped
1/4 cup fresh parsley,
   chopped
1/4 cup fresh dill
   (5 tsp. dried)
1/8 tsp. freshly ground
   pepper

1. Steam potatoes until tender. Cool slightly and cut into quarters.
2. Mix together vinegar and sugar. Heat until sugar is melted and
   vinegar is clear. Remove from heat.
3. Whisk in mustard, yogurt, and mayonnaise. Pour over potatoes.
4. Add bacon, onions, parsley, dill, and pepper. Toss gently until
   well coated. Serve slightly warm.

Dilly Potato Salad

Janet Melvin
Heritage Restaurant Gardens and Gifts
Cincinnati, OH

Makes 10 servings

5 Tbsp. tarragon vinegar
1 Tbsp. minced shallots
2 Tbsp. Dijon mustard
1/2 tsp. curry powder
3/4 cup olive oil
2 Tbsp. minced capers
1/2 cup minced carrots
1/2 cup minced celery
6 Tbsp. minced sweet
  gherkin pickles
1/2 cup minced green onions,
  including tops
1/2 cup minced green
  bell pepper

1/2 cup minced red
  bell pepper
1/4 cup minced fresh
  parsley (5 tsp. dried)
1/4 cup minced fresh
  dill (5 tsp. dried)
1 Tbsp. salt
1 tsp. black pepper
1 gallon cold water
1/4 cup salt
2 lb. new red potatoes,
  cut in 1" cubes

1. Mix together vinegar, shallots, mustard, and curry powder in food processor.
2. Slowly add olive oil to make a dressing.
3. Add capers, carrots, celery, pickles, onions, peppers, parsley, dill, salt, and pepper. Pulse quickly to combine. Add more oil and vinegar if needed until the mixture becomes a thick dressing.
4. Combine water and salt. Add potatoes, making sure there is enough water to cover them. Bring to boil. Turn down and cook just above a simmer until potatoes are barely fork-tender. Be careful not to overcook. Drain.
5. While potatoes are still warm, combine them with enough of the dressing to lightly coat them. Cover and refrigerate. Refrigerate extra dressing for future use.

Garbanzo Bean Herb Salad

Jacqui Savage and Norma Constien
Golden Creek Herbs
Perkins, OK

Makes 4 servings

1 clove garlic, minced
4¹/2 Tbsp. chopped fresh
   spearmint (1¹/2 Tbsp. dried)
2¹/2 Tbsp. fresh lime juice

1 Tbsp. white wine vinegar
3 Tbsp. olive oil
salt to taste
3 cups garbanzo beans,
   drained

1. Mix together all ingredients except beans. Whisk well.
2. Pour over beans and stir to coat. Let stand for 30 minutes or longer before serving.
3. Serve on a bed of lettuce.

Black Bean and Potato Salad

Harriette Johnson
and Dianna Johnson-Fiergola
Mustard Seed Herbs & Everlastings
Spring Valley, WI

Makes 6-8 servings

1 lb. tiny new red potatoes
15-oz. can black beans, drained
1 lb. smoked salmon, flaked
3 Tbsp. fresh dill, minced
   (3 tsp. dried)
¹/2 cup finely minced parsley
   (3 Tbsp. dried)
1 Tbsp. capers
1 large leek, chopped

4 Tbsp. herb vinegar
   (dill is especially good)
¹/4 cup olive oil
2 Tbsp. lemon juice
1 tsp. grainy mustard
1 tsp. Dijon mustard
salt to taste
freshly ground pepper
   to taste

1. Cook new potatoes in their skins. Cool and quarter.
2. To potatoes, add beans, salmon, dill, parsley, capers, and leek. Mix gently.
3. Mix together vinegar, oil, lemon juice, mustards, salt, and pepper. Add to salad and toss lightly.

Five Bean Salad

Jacoba Baker & Reenie Baker Sandsted
Baker's Acres
Groton, NY

Makes 8-10 servings

12 oz. frozen baby lima beans
12 oz. frozen green beans
12 oz. frozen yellow beans
14-oz. can kidney beans,
   drained and rinsed
1 can ceci beans, drained
1-2 red onions, cut in rings
3/4 cup sugar
3/4 cup oil
3/4 cup wine vinegar

1 Tbsp. chopped fresh
   parsley (1 tsp. dried)
1 Tbsp. chopped fresh
   oregano (1 tsp. dried)
1 1/2 tsp. chopped fresh
   basil (1/2 tsp. dried)
1 1/2 tsp. chopped fresh
   thyme (1/2 tsp. dried)
1/2 tsp. salt

1. Cook lima beans, green beans, and yellow beans until tender. Cool.
2. Combine cooked beans with kidney beans, ceci beans, and onions.
3. Mix together sugar, oil, vinegar, parsley, oregano, basil, thyme, and salt. Toss with beans. Marinate overnight.

Italian Olive Salad

Donna Treloar
Harmony
Gaston, IN

Makes 25 servings

21-oz. jar green olives,
   drained
4 6-oz. cans ripe olives,
   drained
2 15-oz. cans garbanzo beans,
   drained
2 1/2 cups Harmony Italian
   Dressing (see page 13)

2 4-oz. jars pimentos,
   drained
2 large onions, cut in
   chunks, then separated
1 quart pepperoncini
   peppers, drained

1. Mix together all ingredients. Stir gently to coat with dressing.
2. Marinate in refrigerator for at least 8 hours. Stir occasionally.

*Note: This works well as a carry-in dish for picnics. If you don't
need a large amount, you can cut the recipe in half or in fourths.*

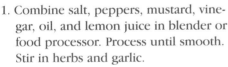

Marinated Vegetable Salad

Gerry Janus
Vileniki—An Herb Farm
Montdale, PA

Makes 6 servings

pinch of salt
1/4 tsp. freshly ground pepper
dash of cayenne pepper
1 tsp. Dijon mustard
3 tsp. tarragon vinegar
1/2 cup olive oil
1 Tbsp. lemon juice
1 tsp. chopped fresh tarragon
1 tsp. chopped fresh lemon balm

4 tsp. chopped fresh chives
2 Tbsp. chopped fresh
   parsley
2 cloves garlic, minced
1 small head cauliflower
1 small bunch broccoli
2 carrots

1. Combine salt, peppers, mustard, vinegar, oil, and lemon juice in blender or
   food processor. Process until smooth.
   Stir in herbs and garlic.
2. Separate cauliflower and broccoli into serv-
   ing-size pieces. Cut carrots into 3"-long,
   thin sticks. Steam vegetables lightly, until
   crisp tender.
3. Pour dressing over hot vegetables. Stir to
   coat well.
4. Refrigerate for several hours, turning vegetables occasionally.

Southwest Carrot Salad

Shari Jensen
Crestline Enterprises
Fountain, CO

Makes 4 servings

1 medium onion, peeled
  and diced
3 cups sliced carrots, cooked
  just until crisp-tender
1/3 cup white wine vinegar
2/3 cup olive oil
1 tsp. dry minced garlic
1 tsp. sugar
1 tsp. lemon juice

1 1/2 Tbsp. chopped fresh
  dill (1/2 Tbsp. dried)
1 1/2 Tbsp. chopped fresh
  cilantro
1 1/2 Tbsp. chopped Mexican
  oregano (1/2 Tbsp. dried)
salt to taste
pepper to taste

1. Mix together onion and carrots.
2. Mix together remaining ingredients. Pour over carrots and toss
   to mix. Cover.
3. Refrigerate for 24 hours before serving. Will keep in the refrigerator for up to 2 weeks.

Freezer Slaw with Lovage

Jacqueline Swift
Rainbow's End Herbs
Perrysburg, NY

Makes 1 1/2 quarts

1 medium head green cabbage,
  shredded (about 10 cups)
1 carrot, shredded
1 red bell pepper, diced
1 tsp. salt
1 cup white wine vinegar

2 cups sugar or less,
  according to taste
1 tsp. celery seeds
1 tsp. mustard seeds
1/2 cup fresh lovage leaves
  and tender stems

1. Combine cabbage, carrot, pepper, and salt. Let stand for one hour.
2. In saucepan, combine vinegar, sugar, celery seeds, and mustard seeds. Boil one minute. Cool.

3. Drain vegetables. Mix together vegetables, cooked dressing, and lovage. Stir gently. Chill.
4. Serve (the slaw will keep up to one week in the refrigerator), or freeze for later use.

Note: This is a good way to use the cabbage your garden produces beyond what you are able to use immediately.

Norm's Coleslaw

Kim Snyder
Kim's Kakes, Kuttings, and Kandles, too!
Ivesdale, IL

Makes 8 servings

large head of cabbage,
   chopped fine
2-3 carrots, grated
1 cup sugar
1/4 tsp. garlic salt
1/4 tsp. pepper

1/4 tsp. dill seeds or
   celery seeds
1/2 cup herbal vinegar
   (basil, rosemary,
   or tarragon)
1/3 cup oil

1. Mix together cabbage and carrots.
2. Sprinkle sugar, garlic salt, pepper, and dill seeds over cabbage.
3. Pour vinegar over mixture.
4. Stir in oil. Mix gently until sugar is dissolved.

Variation: Use one small head of red cabbage and one small head of green cabbage for a colorful slaw.

Barley, Corn, and Rosemary Salad

Brandon Brown
Brown's Edgewood Gardens
Orlando, FL

Makes 10 servings

6 cups water
1/4 tsp. salt
1 cup pearl barley
2 cups corn, steamed
   for 5 minutes
1/2 cup chopped fresh rosemary
1/2 cup minced green onion

1 red bell pepper, diced
1/4 tsp. chopped fresh
   parsley
1/4 cup olive oil
2 Tbsp. fresh lemon juice
2 Tbsp. vinegar
   (plum vinegar is
   especially good)

1. Bring water and salt to boil. Rinse barley and add to water. Simmer 40 minutes. Cool.
2. Stir in corn, rosemary, onion, bell pepper, and parsley.
3. Mix together oil, lemon juice, and vinegar. Pour over barley and vegetables and mix well.

Tabouli

Jacoba Baker & Reenie Baker Sandsted
Baker's Acres
Groton, NY

Makes 6-8 servings

1 cup dry bulgur
2 cups water
1/2 cup chopped scallions
2 large tomatoes, chopped
1/4 cup olive oil
1 tsp. salt

1 heaping tsp.
   crushed fresh garlic
1/2 cup chopped fresh mint
2 cups chopped fresh parsley
1/4 cup lemon or lime juice
freshly ground pepper
   to taste

1. Soak bulgur in water for 2 hours, or until all water is absorbed.
2. Stir in remaining ingredients, allow flavors to blend, and serve.

Wild Rice Salad with Mint

Dawn Ranck
Harrisonburg, VA

Makes 6-8 servings

1/2 cup uncooked white rice	1 cup yellow raisins
1/2 cup raw wild rice	1 cup chopped pecans
5 1/2 cups chicken broth	1/4 cup oil
4 scallions, sliced thin	1/3 cup orange juice
1/4 cup chopped fresh mint	1 tsp. salt
grated rind of 1 orange	1/4 tsp. pepper

1. Mix together white rice, wild rice, and chicken broth. Simmer uncovered for 40-50 minutes. Rice should not be too soft. Drain.
2. Mix together remaining ingredients. Gently stir into rice mixture.
3. Let stand at room temperature for 2 hours before serving, or refrigerate for at least 8 hours before serving.

Tuna Salad with Lovage

Judy Kehs
Cricket Hill Herb Farm
Rowley, MA

Makes 4 servings

9-oz. can white tuna, drained and flaked	lettuce
1/2 cup cottage cheese	sliced tomatoes
2 Tbsp. grated horseradish	sliced cucumbers
2 Tbsp. chopped fresh lovage leaves (2 tsp. dried)	bread
	fresh parsley sprigs
	lemon slices

1. Mix together tuna, cottage cheese, horseradish, and lovage.
2. Serve on lettuce, garnished with sliced tomatoes and cucumbers, or serve as open-faced sandwiches. Sprinkle with fresh parsley and serve with slices of lemon.

Herbed Tuna Salad

Lorraine Hamilton
Lorraine's Herb Garden
Neelyton, PA

Makes 4 servings

6½-oz. can tuna, drained
½ cup chopped celery,
   or ¼ cup minced fresh lovage
2 hard-boiled eggs, chopped
3 Tbsp. minced fresh herbs
   (1 Tbsp. dried)—choose dill,
   thyme, chives, parsley, or a
   combination of any of those

1-2 Tbsp. herb vinegar
   (chive, floral, dill and
   lemon balm, lemon
   thyme, or tarragon)
¼ cup mayonnaise
herb flowers or
   nasturtium leaves

1. Mix together all ingredients.
2. Chill at least one hour.
3. Garnish with herbs or herb flowers or roll in nasturtium leaves
   and hold together with toothpicks.

Spring Tuna Salad

Carol Frank
Summer Kitchen Herbs
Allenton, WI

Makes 4 servings

6½-oz. can tuna, drained
2 hard-boiled eggs, cut into
   small pieces
1 fresh French sorrel leaf,
   chopped
3 fresh lovage leaves, chopped
1 sprig tarragon leaves, chopped
8 chive stalks, chopped

1 cup cooked elbow
   macaroni
salt to taste
pepper to taste
½ to ¾ cup mayonnaise or
   salad dressing
½ tsp. prepared mustard

Mix together all ingredients. Serve on lettuce leaves.

Fusilli with Tomatoes and Tuna

Harriette Johnson &
Dianna Johnson Fiergola
Mustard Seed Herbs
Spring Valley, WI

Makes 6-8 servings

1 lb. fusilli
2 cups diced red & yellow
   tomatoes
2 6¹/₂ -oz. cans tuna
³/₄ cup chopped fresh basil

1 Tbsp. capers
¹/₂ tsp. salt
¹/₂ tsp. freshly ground pepper
¹/₃ cup basil vinegar
¹/₄ cup olive oil

1. Cook, drain, and chill fusilli.
2. Stir in tomatoes, tuna, basil, capers, salt, and pepper.
3. Stir together vinegar and oil. Toss with salad.
4. Refrigerate 30 minutes before serving.

Shrimp Salad

Harriette Johnson & Dianna Johnson-Fiergola
Mustard Seed Herbs & Everlastings
Spring Valley, WI

Makes 12-14 servings

8 oz. cooked shrimp
3 tomatoes, diced
2 cucumbers, diced
1 red onion, sliced
6-oz. can black olives, sliced
2 tsp. chopped fresh dill
2 tsp. chopped fresh parsley

³/₄ cup Italian dressing or
   ¹/₃ cup herbal vinegar
   mixed with ¹/₄ cup olive oil
freshly ground black pepper
   to taste
salt to taste
4-6 oz. feta cheese, crumbled

Mix together all ingredients in order listed and then serve immediately.

Curried Seafood Rice Salad

Toni Anderson
Cedarbrook Herb Farm
Sequim, WA

Makes 10-12 servings

Dressing:
1/2 cup mayonnaise
1/2 cup plain yogurt
3 Tbsp. chopped fresh
  spearmint (1 tsp. dried)
1 Tbsp. lemon juice
1 tsp. curry powder
1/2 tsp. salt
1 1/2 tsp. fresh basil
  (1/2 tsp. dried)
dash of cayenne

3 cups cooked brown rice
8 oz. smoked salmon, flaked
1 cup sliced celery
10-oz. pkg. petite frozen
  peas, thawed
1/2 cup sliced green onion,
  including some tops
1/4 cup diced red bell pepper
1 pint cherry tomatoes,
  cut in half
3 hard-boiled eggs, chopped
1/4 lb. small salad shrimp
fresh spearmint sprigs

1. Mix together all dressing ingredients. Chill for 3 hours.
2. Combine rice, salmon, celery, peas, onions, pepper, and tomatoes. Mix well. Stir in eggs. Mix together lightly.
3. Chill for 3 hours.
4. Pour dressing over salad and gently mix. Garnish with shrimp and fresh spearmint sprigs.

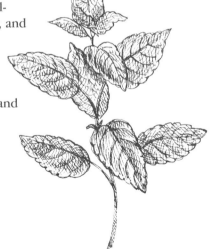

Jill's Dill-icious Chicken Salad

Betty Leonard
Hampton Herbs
New Carlisle, OH

Makes 6-8 servings

1 lb. lettuce, shredded
1¹/2 lbs. (about 2 cups)
  cooked chicken breast, cubed
2 cups dry three-color pasta,
  prepared according to
  package directions
1 medium cucumber, sliced

1 medium red onion,
  sliced thin
10 oz. frozen peas, thawed
2 cups salad dressing
2-3 Tbsp. fresh dill
1 cup shredded
  cheddar cheese

1. Layer ingredients, except cheese, in order given.
2. Refrigerate for several hours until ready to serve.
3. Toss well. Sprinkle cheese over top.

Cold Ham and Chicken Potato Salad

Judy Kehs
Cricket Hill Herb Farm
Rowley, MA

Makes 4 servings

2 lbs. potatoes
1 cup chicken broth
2 cups chopped cooked chicken
2 cups chopped cooked ham
4 oz. sour cream
5 Tbsp. chopped fresh dill
  (1¹/2 Tbsp. dried)

1 cup mayonnaise
2 Tbsp. dark mustard
2 green onions, chopped
1 green pepper, chopped
cucumber slices
2 hard-boiled eggs, sliced

1. Cook potatoes in chicken broth until tender. Cool, peel, and cut in small cubes.
2. Combine chicken, ham, sour cream, dill, mayonnaise, mustard, onions, and pepper. Mix well.
3. Add potatoes and toss. Chill.
4. Serve garnished with sliced cucumbers and hard-boiled egg slices.

Tarragon Chicken Salad

Harriette Johnson &
Dianna Johnson-Fiergola
Mustard Seed Herbs and Everlastings
Spring Valley, WI

Makes 4-6 servings

1 lb. diced chicken or
  turkey breast
1 cup red grapes
1 cup green grapes
2 cups pea pods, cut in pieces
1 cup fresh tarragon leaves
  (5 Tbsp. dried)
1 cup mayonnaise

1 cup plain yogurt
3 Tbsp. lemon juice
3 Tbsp. tarragon vinegar
1 tsp. salt
freshly ground pepper
  to taste
salad greens
1 cup broken cashews

1. Mix together chicken, grapes, pea pods, and tarragon.
2. Mix together mayonnaise, yogurt, lemon juice, vinegar, salt, and pepper. Pour over chicken mixture and gently toss until well coated.
3. Serve on salad greens and top with cashews.

Strawberry Chicken Salad

Jan Mast
The Herb Shop
Lititz, PA

Makes 4-6 servings

1 lb. fresh spinach,
  torn into pieces
half head romaine lettuce
half head red leaf lettuce

Dressing:
1/3 cup oil
1/2 cup strawberry vinegar
1 Tbsp. sugar
1 tsp. poppy seeds
2 Tbsp. orange juice

3 chicken breasts, cooked
  and cubed
1 quart strawberries, sliced
1 honeydew melon, balled

1/2 tsp. grated onion
1 tsp. dry mustard
freshly grated lemon rind
1 tsp. fresh parsley

26

1. Toss spinach and lettuces together. Toss in chicken, strawberries, and melon balls.
2. Mix together all dressing ingredients. Pour dressing over salad just before serving.

Basil Cream

Judy C. Jensen
Fairlight Gardens
Auburn, WA

Makes 2¹/2 cups

¹/2 cup fresh basil leaves	**2 Tbsp. Dijon mustard**
1-2 cloves garlic	**1 cup nonfat plain yogurt**
¹/3 cup olive oil	**salt to taste**
2¹/2 Tbsp. white wine vinegar	**pepper to taste**

1. In food processor or blender, chop basil and garlic.
2. Pour in oil, vinegar, and mustard. Process.
3. Stir in yogurt. Season with salt and pepper.
4. Serve over pasta, chicken, or as a vegetable dip.

Dill Sauce

Jane D. Look
Pineapple Hill Herbs and More
Mapleton, IL

Makes 1+ cup

2 Tbsp. butter or margarine	**1 Tbsp. chopped fresh dill**
2 Tbsp. flour	**(1 tsp. dried), or**
¹/2 tsp. salt	**¹/2 tsp. dried dill seeds**
1 cup milk	

1. Melt butter over low heat. Stir in flour.
2. Add salt, dill, and milk. Slowly bring to boil, stirring constantly. Reduce heat and cook until thickened, about 5 minutes.
3. Serve over rice, noodles, macaroni, boiled potatoes, or fish.

Lizard Sauce

Barb Perry
Lizard Lick Organic Herbs
Huron, TN

Makes approximately 2 cups

1 cup cayenne peppers or a mixture of hot red peppers, with stems removed	6 cloves garlic
1 medium red or yellow onion, chopped	1 cup apple cider vinegar
	2 tsp. salt
	1/2 cup honey

1. Put peppers, onion, and garlic in blender. Chop finely.
2. Heat vinegar, salt, and honey until well mixed.
3. Pour hot vinegar mixture over peppers, onions, and garlic. Cover and process on high speed until smooth. If too thick to pour, add more vinegar.
4. Store in glass shaker bottles.

Note: This is a hot and lively pepper sauce to use anytime you want a peppery flavor.

Basic Basil Pesto

Charles R. Fogleman
Ashcombe Farm and Greenhouses
Mechanicsburg, PA
Judy C. Jensen
Fairlight Gardens
Auburn, WA

Makes 1 cup

2 cups fresh basil leaves	1/4 cup pine nuts or walnuts
2 cloves garlic	1/2 cup olive oil
1/2 cup freshly grated Parmesan cheese	salt and pepper to taste

1. Place basil in food processor or blender and chop.
2. Add garlic, cheese, and nuts. Process to mix.

3. Add olive oil, salt, and pepper and process to desired consistency.
4. Allow to stand for 5-10 minutes before serving on your favorite crackers, pasta, or raw vegetables.

Note: Can be kept in refrigerator for up to 1 week. Freezes best when you leave the garlic out and add it just before serving.

Herbed Salad Dressing

Lynea Weatherly
The Herb College
San Antonio, TX

Makes 3/4 + cup

2 Tbsp. dried tarragon	3 Tbsp. dried parsley
2 Tbsp. dried dill seeds	1 Tbsp. dried mustard
1 Tbsp. dried rosemary	1 Tbsp. vege-sal (optional)
3 Tbsp. dried chives	1 Tbsp. dried basil

1. Mix together all ingredients until well blended.
2. To serve, add 1 Tbsp. herb mix to 6 Tbsp. olive oil and 2 Tbsp. apple cider vinegar. Spray on or pour over salad greens or sliced tomatoes.

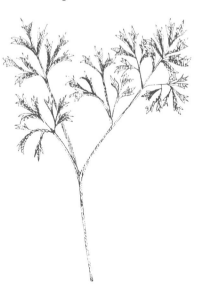

Herbed Cream Cheese Salad Dressing

Judy and Don Jensen
Fairlight Gardens
Auburn, WA

Makes 2¹/2 cups

8-oz. pkg. cream cheese,
  softened
¹/2 cup sour cream
¹/2 cup chopped fresh parsley
  leaves (3 Tbsp. dried)
¹/2 cup chopped fresh dill
  sprigs without stems
  (3 Tbsp. dried)

¹/2 cup chopped fresh
  chives (3 Tbsp. dried)
1 Tbsp. white wine vinegar
¹/4 cup vegetable oil
2 tsp. Worcestershire sauce
¹/2 cup milk
salt to taste
pepper to taste

1.Blend together all ingredients in food processor or mixer.
  Process until smooth.
2. Add more milk if needed to use as salad dressing.

Creamy Basil Dressing

Wendy Harrington
Harvest Herb Company
Malone, NY

Makes 2 cups

¹/4 cup firmly packed fresh
  basil leaves
1 cup mayonnaise
¹/2 cup sour cream
3 green onions, chopped
1 clove garlic, minced

3 Tbsp. herbal vinegar
2 Tbsp. chopped fresh chives
1 tsp. Worcestershire sauce
¹/2 tsp. dry mustard
freshly ground pepper
  to taste

1. Combine all ingredients in blender or food processor. Blend
  until smooth. Refrigerate for up to one week.
2. Spread over fresh tomatoes, pour over mixed green salads, or
  use as a dip.

Dill Salad Dressing

Jane D. Look
Pineapple Hill Herbs and More
Mapleton, IL

Makes 2 cups

1/4 cup vegetable oil
1 cup sour cream
2 Tbsp. vinegar
1 Tbsp. chopped fresh dill
   (1 tsp. dried), or to taste

4 eggs
1 tsp. salt
1 tsp. garlic powder
1 tsp. onion powder
1 tsp. ground pepper

1. Mix together all ingredients in blender.
2. Refrigerate until ready to use.

Dilled Cucumber Salad Dressing

Charlotte Chandler
Honey of an Herb Farm
Walton, WV

Makes 2 cups

1 large cucumber, seeded
   and chopped
2 Tbsp. chopped fresh dill
1 Tbsp. extra-virgin olive oil
2 tsp. lemon juice

1 tsp. white wine
   Worcestershire sauce
2/3 cup plain low-fat yogurt
1/4 tsp. salt
1/4 tsp. ground white pepper

1. In food processor, blend cucumber, dill, olive oil, lemon juice, and Worcestershire until cucumber is finely chopped.
2. Add yogurt, salt, and pepper. Process until smooth.
3. Refrigerate until ready to serve.
4. Use as a dip for steamed or raw vegetables or pour over salad greens.

Quick Vinaigrette

Carol Ebbighausen-Smith
C&C Herb Farm
Spokane, WA

Makes 1 cup

1 Tbsp. chopped fresh basil
(1 tsp. dried)
1 Tbsp. chopped fresh chives
(1 tsp. dried)
1 Tbsp. chopped fresh parsley
(1 tsp. dried)
1 Tbsp. chopped fresh tarragon
(1 tsp. dried)

1 Tbsp. chopped fresh
lemon thyme (1 tsp. dried)
1/4 cup cider vinegar
1/4 cup water
1/2 cup olive oil

1. Mix together basil, chives, parsley, tarragon, and lemon thyme.
2. Mix together vinegar and water. Heat just to boiling point.
3. Pour over herbs. Whisk together. Let stand for 5 minutes.
4. Whisk in olive oil. Allow to cool.
5. Serve over salads, roasted vegetables, fresh fruit, or baked fish.

About the Authors

Dawn J. Ranck is an advocate of bringing herbs to everyone's kitchens, not just to the cooking artists'.

A resident of Harrisonburg, Virginia, she is also the co-author of *A Quilter's Christmas Cookbook.*

Phyllis Pellman Good, Lancaster, Pennsylvania, has had her hand in many cookbooks—among them, *The Best of Amish Cooking, Recipes from Central Market,* and *The Best of Mennonite Fellowship Meals.*